This book belongs to …

Debbie

FOZ ILion

OXFORD
UNIVERSITY PRESS

Oxford University Press is a department of the University of Oxford.
It furthers the University's objective of excellence in research, scholarship,
and education by publishing worldwide. Oxford is a registered trade mark
ofOxford University Press in the UK and in certain other countries

ISBN: 978-0-19-273649-9

1 3 5 7 9 10 8 6 4 2

Paper used in the production of this book is a natural, recyclable product made
from wood grown in sustainable forests. The manufacturing process conforms
to the environmental regulations of the country of origin.

Acknowledgements:
Series Editor: Annemarie Young

READ WITH
Biff,
Chip &
Kipper

Kipper's Rhymes
and Other Stories

OXFORD
UNIVERSITY PRESS

Tips for Reading Together

Children learn best when they are having fun.

- Tell your child that they are going to help Biff read captions and look for things in the pictures.
- Ask your child to read the captions and sentences on the left hand page. Then ask them to match them to the correct picture on the right hand page.
- Don't forget that if you talk about letter sounds, for example 'b', you should say *buh*, not *bee*. You can listen to the letter sounds on www.oxfordowl.co.uk.
- Give lots of praise as your child reads with you and does the activities.
- Play the game on page 26 to help the muddy pup get to the bath.

Have fun!

Find the spider hidden in every picture.

This book practises these letter sounds:

s a t p i n m d g o c ck

e u r h b f l v ff ll ss

For more hints and tips on helping your child become a successful and enthusiastic reader look at our website www.oxfordowl.co.uk.

Biff's Fun Phonics

Written by Annemarie Young,
based on the original characters
created by Roderick Hunt and Alex Brychta
Illustrated by Nick Schon

OXFORD

UNIVERSITY PRESS

 Read the two captions.
Can you match each caption
to its picture?

a cap on a peg

a cup and a mug

Read the two captions.
Can you match each caption
to its picture?

cod in a pan

carrots in a pot

 Read the sentences. Which one
matches the picture?

Hit the bell.

Fill the pot.

 Read the captions. Can you find the rat and the hat in the picture?

a rat as big as a cat

a red hat in a red bag

15

Read these captions. Can you match the captions to the pictures?

red on the rug

mess on the mat

 Read the sentences. Can you find the rabbit and the pup in the picture?

The rabbit is in the hut.

The pup is in the mud.

19

 Read the sentences. Which
one matches the picture?

Get off the bus.

Get a hug and a kiss.

21

 Read the sentences. Which one matches the picture?

A nut on the bag.

Get on top of the rock.

 Read the sentences. Can you find the rabbit and the duck in the picture?

The rabbit is at the vet.

The duck is on top.

25

Muddy maze

Help the muddy pup get to the bath.

Tips for Reading Together

Children learn best when they are having fun.

- Tell your child that they are going to help Kipper read some fun rhymes and play 'I spy'.
- Ask your child to read the rhymes on the left hand page. Then ask them to find the objects in the scene on the right hand page.
- Once they have done this, ask them to find other ryhming objects in the picture.
- Don't forget that if you talk about letter sounds, for example 'b', you should say *buh*, not *bee*. You can listen to the letter sounds on www.oxfordowl.co.uk.
- Give lots of praise as your child reads with you and does the activities.
- Play the game on page 48 to help Dad find his way home in the fog.

Have fun!

Find the robin hidden in every picture.

This book practises these letter sounds:
s a t p i n m d g o c k ck
e u r h b f l j w ff ll ss

For more hints and tips on helping your child become a successful and enthusiastic reader look at our website www.oxfordowl.co.uk.

Kipper's Rhymes

Written by Annemarie Young,
based on the original characters
created by Roderick Hunt and Alex Brychta
Illustrated by Alex Brychta

OXFORD
UNIVERSITY PRESS

Read these rhyming words and
find them in the picture.

A bug in a mug.

A jug on the rug.

What else can you
find in the picture that
rhymes with **mug**?

hug, slug

Read these rhyming words and
find them in the picture.

A wet pet!

A fan and a can.

What other things
can you find in the
picture that rhyme with
pet and **can**?

jet, net, man, pan

Read these rhyming words and
find them in the picture.

Less mess, Biff!

Ted is on the bed.

What things can you
find in the picture that
rhyme with **sock**?

clock, rock

Read these rhyming words and
find them in the picture.

Hop to the top.

Bill is on the hill.

What else can you find in the picture that rhymes with **top**?

mop, pop

37

Read these rhyming words and
find them in the picture.

A dog on a log.

Huff and puff!

What else can you
find in the picture that
rhymes with **dog**?

fog, jog, bog

Read these rhyming words and
find them in the picture.

Jack and his backpack.

Mack in a sack.

What else can you
find in the picture that
rhymes with **sack**?

track

41

Read these rhyming words and
find them in the picture.

The hen is in a pen.

The egg is on
a peg.

What else can you
find in the picture that
rhymes with **pen**
and **peg**?

ten, men, leg

Read these rhyming words and
find them in the picture.

A ticket in a pocket.

A rocket in a bucket.

What can you
find in the picture that
rhymes with **duck**?

truck

45

Read these rhyming words and
find them in the picture.

Pat a cat.

A rat sat on a mat.

What else can you find in the picture that rhymes with **cat**?

hat, bat

47

Maze haze

Help Dad get home in the fog.

Tips for Reading Together

This book has two stories: *The Pancake* (page 50) and *Floppy Floppy* (page 61).

- For each story, look through the pictures so your child can see what the story is about.
- Read the story to your child, placing your finger under each word as you read.
- Read the story again and encourage your child to join in.
- Give lots of praise as your child reads with you.
- Do the fun activity with your child.

Children enjoy re-reading stories and this helps to build their confidence.

Have fun!

After you have read *Floppy Floppy* find the caterpillar in every picture.

This book includes these common words:

the   no

For more hints and tips on helping your child become a successful and enthusiastic reader look at our website www.oxfordowl.co.uk.

The Pancake

Written by Roderick Hunt
Illustrated by Alex Brychta

The frying pan,

the flour,

the eggs,

the milk,

the butter,

the pancake.

57

The pancake race!

Talk about the story

What went into the pancake?

Who stirred the pancake mixture?

What did Dad do with the pancake?

What is your favourite pancake filling?

Spot the difference

Find the five differences in the two pictures.

Floppy Floppy

Written by Roderick Hunt

Illustrated by Alex Brychta

Oh, Floppy!

No, Floppy!

Oh, Floppy!

No, Floppy!

Floppy Floppy.

Talk about the story

Match the shadows

Can you match the pictures of Floppy with
the shadows of Floppy?

This book has two stories: *A Good Trick* (page 72) and *Fun at the Beach* (page 83).

- For each story, look through the pictures so your child can see what the story is about.
- Read the story to your child, placing your finger under each word as you read.
- Read the story again and encourage your child to join in.
- Give lots of praise as your child reads with you.
- Do the fun activity with your child.

Children enjoy re-reading stories and this helps to build their confidence.

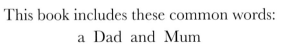

After you have read *Fun at the Beach*, find the butterfly in every picture.

This book includes these common words:
a Dad and Mum

For more hints and tips on helping your child become a successful and enthusiastic reader look at our website www.oxfordowl.co.uk.

A Good Trick

Written by Roderick Hunt
Illustrated by Alex Brychta

A rug,

a sheet,

a big box,

a little box,

Kipper!

Talk about the story

Spot the difference

Find the five differences in the two pictures.

Fun at the Beach

Written by Roderick Hunt
Illustrated by Alex Brychta

Dad and Mum.

Mum and Dad.

Kipper, Chip and Biff.

Kipper, Biff and Dad.

Mum, Chip and Floppy.

Chip, Biff and Kipper.

Dad and Floppy.

Oh Floppy!

Talk about the story

Spot the pair

Find the identical pair.

Read with Biff, Chip & Kipper

The UK's best-selling home reading series

Phonics stories help children practise their sounds and letters, as they learn to do in school.

First Stories have been specially written to provide practice in reading everyday language.

Phonics   First Stories

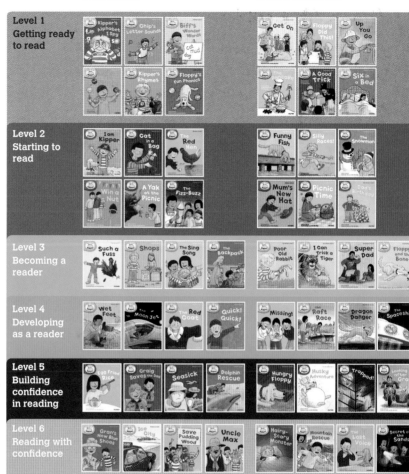

Level 1 Getting ready to read

Level 2 Starting to read

Level 3 Becoming a reader

Level 4 Developing as a reader

Level 5 Building confidence in reading

Level 6 Reading with confidence

Read with Biff, Chip and Kipper Collections:

2 Phonics and 2 First Stories in every collection

Phonics support

Flashcards are a really fun way to practise phonics and build reading skills. **Age 3+**

My Phonics Kit is designed to support you and your child as you practise phonics together at home. It includes stickers, workbooks, interactive eBooks, support for parents and more! **Age 5+**

Read Write Inc. Phonics: A range of fun rhyming stories to support decoding skills. **Age 4+**

Songbirds Phonics: Lively and engaging phonics stories from former Children's Laureate, Julia Donaldson. **Age 4+**

Helping your child's learning with free eBooks, essential tips and fun activities
www.oxfordowl.co.uk